VIETNAM IN VERSE

written and illustrated by

GARRY A. NOLAND

VIETNAM IN VERSE

written and illustrated by

GARRY A. NOLAND

DORRANCE
PUBLISHING CO
EST. 1920
PITTSBURGH, PENNSYLVANIA 15238

Dorrance Publishing Co
585 Alpha Drive, Suite 103
Pittsburgh, PA 15238
Visit our website at *www.dorrancebookstore.com*

ISBN: 978-1-6461-0519-9
eISBN: 978-1-6461-0655-4

VIETNAM IN VERSE

BY

GARRY NOLAND

THE WAR POET FROM EAST TENNESSEE

THE MAN WHO LOVES HIS COUNTRY

AND HATES THE POLITICS OF WAR

frontispiece

The photo in the frontispiece was taken from the National Archives and was made by a Marine Corps photographer on or about November 1st, 1943 in Bougainville, an island in the Solomon Islands. My Father, D.A. Noland, had just delivered a truckload of supplies to the Marines protecting the airfield. Word came down that a Japanese fleet was nearing the area. The US fleet put out to sea, leaving my Dad and several other sailors as guests of the 3rd Marine Division. Dad shed his Navy uniform and was issued Marines Corps battle dress and a 1903 Springfield Rifle. For two weeks until his ship returned, he was adopted by the Marines and was well cared for by the amused young men. Receiving on the job training as an infantryman, he helped repel several suicide charges. According to Dad, "The Marines were some of the biggest fellars I ever saw." My father is the one in front wearing leggings.

VIETNAM IN VERSE

MY WAR STORIES IN RHYMED COUPLETS

GARRY A. NOLAND

DEDICATION

This endeavor is dedicated to the memory of my father, D.A. Noland, and all the other unsung heroes of all the wars who courageously defended our great nation. These forgotten ones have received little or no recognition in their lifetimes. Many were wounded physically and mentally with no record that their injuries occurred. No recorded treatment for wounds equals no Purple Heart or recognition for their sacrifices. The fog of war can be mass confusion. Survival and the mission take precedence over record keeping. In many cases there were no living witnesses to their heroism.

These are my Vietnam War Stories in the form of pithy, sardonic poems. Poetry is to prose as brandy is to wine. Rhymed couplets are my vehicle of choice for conveying my dark humor and a sense of futility while still maintaining patriotism and loyalty to my bothers in arms. Compiling these has been cathartic and painful.

I drew the pencil drawings, some from photos, to illustrate my poems without having copyright issues. They are both literal and symbolic representations of my observations and feelings. I think of them as single frames cut from the reel of my autobiographical movie.

Each of my drawings has my initials, GAN, in the lower right corner. The act of making a drawing was in itself therapeutic.

Albert Fuerst, my best Army buddy, contributed material for three of these poems. His memory served as "hamburger helper" for my own which suffered from the effects of an artillery barrage (poem 24). Footnotes accompany each poem where necessary to explain military anagrams and jargon.

The names in the poems have been changed, except for Al Fuerst and mine, to protect the guilty and the innocent.

Note to the reader:

These 42 poems were composed over a period of 49 years and are arranged in chronological order starting in 1969 and continuing to 2018. The table of contents is divided into chapters and verses. Chapters are distinctive eras in my military service or life. Verses are the individual poems themselves which relate my war stories and are bittersweet like life itself.

After the passing of my wife in October of 2017, I had a total of four poems which only existed in my head and had been composed years ago. In November of 2017, I visited my old Army buddy, Al Fuerst, who encouraged me to write up all my war stories in the form of poems. It would be an unusual way of preserving them for posterity and sharing them with other vets.

Longtime family friend, Mary Jo Keshock, visited me at my home during early 2018. She suggested that I undertake this mini-tome of poetry as a legacy project so future generations might better understand the Vietnam Vet. After she returned home, I sent her copies of my work as soon as I could write them. She was delighted and offered massive amounts of encouragement to motivate me. With this much needed support, I wrote the other 38 poems from March to December of 2018. It was a great stress reliever. Read slowly, reflect, and enjoy.

ABOUT THE AUTHOR

I am a product of many generations of hard-fisted yeomanry, independent farmers often praised for their sturdiness and loyalty, and have deep working-class roots. Growing up in the foothills of the East Tennessee Smokys and in the shadow of the Cascade Mountains of Washington State, I was at an early age exposed to differing points of view. Political correctness in many areas is not my strongest suit. I am a bit rebellious but my thinking has evolved over the years.

I graduated from Carson Newman College, Jefferson City, Tennessee, in 1970 with a Bachelor of Arts in English and was drafted by the Army in December of that year. After serving as a photo interpreter in Military Intelligence, I attended CNC to garner my teacher certification. Subsequently, I taught elementary and high school until my retirement.

My Service in Vietnam was intellectually stimulating, a perfect match for my temperament, interests, and expertise. While in Phu Bai as a member of a 15 man detachment, I planned air strikes to interdict portions of the Ho Chi Minh Trail. Later in Phu Bai, I worked the night shift using infrared and radar imagery so the night would not entirely belong to the enemy.

At Camp Eagle, near Hue in South Vietnam, I worked in the B-52 Targeting Section, looking for cache sites, Surface to Air Missiles (SAMS), and other signs of enemy activity. On the night and morning of December 23rd – 24th, 1971, Al Fuerst and I were guarding a bunker on the perimeter of Camp Eagle. We were about to be overrun by a sapper team intent on blowing up the helicopters and killing high ranking officers with their satchel charges. Before it could be fired, the machine gun jammed. Al called in artillery from Fire Base Bastogne wiping out the enemy and a large part of my hearing. He deservedly received a Bronze Star for his actions. Forty-seven years later on November 6th, 2018, the appeals board in Washington D.C. decided in favor of my claim for service connected hearing loss.

For the first three months of 1971, I was stationed in Saigon and served as a civil affairs non-commissioned officer. My job was to help distribute American aid to two Saigon orphanages.

Assigned to Fort Bragg, North Carolina for the next year and a half until my separation from the Army, I worked as an image interpreter. Utilizing imagery made by the SR-71 Blackbird spyplane, I contributed to several classified projects.

With the aid of the GI Bill and the support of my wife, I obtained two advanced degrees in Educational Administration and Supervision along with several more subject area endorsements from the University of Tennessee Knoxville. My physics endorsement paved the way for my employment as an astronomy instructor with the UTK Evening School.

As a senior in high school, I won first place in Tennessee for a Fraternal Order of Police sponsored essay contest, "What Law Enforcement Means to My Community". Gatlinburg-Pittman High School received a huge trophy and I got a $300 scholarship. While in college, several of my poems were published in the college newspaper. Additionally, while serving at Fort Bragg in 1972, I won an essay contest sponsored by The Freedoms Foundation at Valley Forge entitled "Freedom Has a Price" and was awarded The George Washington Freedom Medal*.

Sadly, I lost my wife of forty years, Elizabeth, to ALS in October of 2017. She was a beautiful woman endowed with compassion and intelligence.

*Presently, The George Washington Freedom Medal is known as The George Washington Honor Medal.

TABLE OF CONTENTS

VIETNAM in VERSE

QUICK LIST LOCATOR

Chapter 1: Reluctant Soldier 1969 – 1971
Verses (Poems) 1 – 6

1. Pacification

2. Winning the Lottery

3. The Reception Station

4. My Coat of OD Color

5. The Re-up

6. Fort Holabird

There is no viable strategy to win the hearts and minds of the people when you are a hated foreign invader. We still haven't learned that lesson. Do not participate directly in other countrys' civil wars.

PACIFICATION

The M-16 is a thing you need,
To make a commie die and bleed;
Swords are out and rifles are in;
To kill a commie ain't no sin.
Shoot their bodies full of holes,
For the edification of their souls;
Burn their huts, pigs and rice;
Shoot 'em once and stab 'em twice.
It's the beginning of pacification;
Kill all the commies in the heathen nation.
Harry them out – give them no rest;
Kill 'em while they're on the breast.
And to be sure they'll bear no others,
Shoot some holes in their Asian mothers.

Written in 1969 as a reaction to the My Lai massacre and published in the Carson-Newman College paper, the Orange and Blue

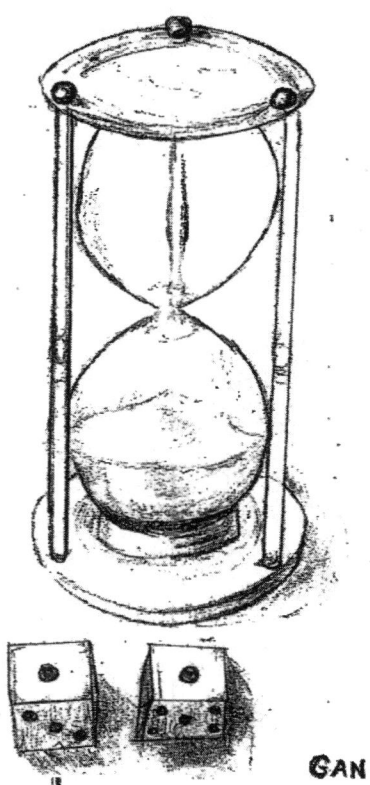

Out of time and out of luck

WINNING THE LOTTERY

It was a special event in Jefferson City;
And throughout the nation elation and pity.
Everyone was for the war;
So it seemed in '64;
Except for Dad and Senator Hatfield.
Said Dad there is nothing to win in Vietnam.
He had fought the Japs in Bougainville
And wanted not his son to be killed
For foreign freedom and freedumber;
To die for corporate greed is a bummer.
He hated the jungle and all it meant
And wanted no one's son there ever sent.
I was a senior that December night,
Watching the television's flickering light.
In the student center at CNC,
There watching the national lottery,
With morbid curiosity to know,
Whether or not I must go,
Off to sacrifice perhaps my life
And never have a family or a wife.
One by one the numbers were drawn,
Knowing our fate before the dawn;
Those elated and those shafted;
Below 195 you're surely drafted.
My number was up at 117,
Shafted to be drafted;

You know what I mean.
I was careful and not a fool,
But I got drunk at that holy school.
My GPA took a hit that night;
I missed honors by a hundredth of a point;
Time for me was out of joint.
I was to be cannon fodder for the fatherland;
Meet my Waterloo or Stalingrad?
So very unhappy were Mom and Dad;
They took it much harder than I;
I'd figure to serve and not to die.
Cronkite* told during Tet of '68;
We had a stalemate and must negotiate.
Mom sent off a husband to fight
And now a son added to her plight.
Begotten by hard-fisted yeomanry,
I cared not a whit for the aristocracy
Who would abort me at 23,
For a war-stimulated economy.
I felt like a Confederate conscript;
A servant of the rich man's contempt;
Fighting to keep his plantation's help.
Whenever it is said they say it right;
It is a rich man's war,
But a poor man's fight.
My involuntary military servitude
Was unconstitutional, mean, and rude.
According to amendment number 13,

I was convicted of a crime;
I had been born at the wrong time.
The night I won the lottery
Will live forever in memory.
I got an extended vacation,
In unnecessary service to the nation.

*Cronkite – Walter Cronkite CBS anchor and the most trusted
newsman in America.

A Drill Sergeant rebuking a recruit

D I Drill Instructor

or

Drill Sergeant

THE RECEPTION STATION

Early in the morning of December 1st,
Hoping for the best but expecting the worst.
Dad took me to the county seat*
On an autumn morning devoid of heat.
I and another draftee boarded a bus
Which to Knoxville soon delivered us.
Naked as jaybirds like a herd of swine,
We quietly walked a bright yellow line
Probed and prodded by medical men,
They checked the mouth and the other end.
I had a prostate without a doubt;
To my tonsils he took the scenic route.
Some brought medical records and x-rays;
Perhaps they were exempted that very day.
They lined us up to be double drafted
Which made us more than doubly sore;
Five were selected for the Jarhead Corps*.
To be inducted I swore a lie;
We all did it not blinking an eye.
We did not enter the obligation
Without hesitation or purpose of evasion.
We had not another choice
And repeated the lie with one voice.
Like a load of convicts prison bound,
We rode quietly off to Louisville town.
After a long, long ride,

We got off that big chartered bus
With a DI standing in among us.
Welcome to the Army, gentlemen, he said;
Then marched us to the mess hall to be fed.
None of us were feeling well;
At Fort Knox it was cold as hell.
My first experience with Army chow,
A frozen part of a long-dead cow,
Burnt on the outside with the inside raw
And ditto for all the hot dogs I saw.
It must be food – it had the looks.
Alas they had no gourmet cooks.
On the average the cooking was great;
We kept it down, everything we ate.
Not long after we were fed,
Off to a barracks we were led.
In civilian clothes we found a bed.
At about half past three we were asleep
When a drunk from Louisville – a sergeant creep
Ended our night and turned on the light.
He tore up our bunks and woolen beds,
Calling us trainees and goddamned dick heads.
He wanted to make for us a private hell;
All his Army training served him so well.
Time to make the best of a bad situation;
Get on with service to an ungrateful nation.

*Jarhead Corps – Army slang for U.S. Marine Corps

*County seat – Sevierville, Tennessee, home town of country
 music singer, songwriter, and actress Dolly Parton

When I was serving in Vietnam, Dolly Parton's "Coat of Many Colors" was popular.

Many years later I wrote this parody to express my feelings about being drafted into the Army and sent on a fool's errand to give up my freedom for those who didn't value their own.

MY COAT OF OD COLOR (ARMY FIELD JACKET)

It was kinda coolish,
Down in the shank of the fall.
I had a pair shoes,
But no Army boots at all.
Then one day Uncle came*
And he said to me:
"Boy, you can shoot,
'cause you're from Tennessee."
He taught me to drill and march;
Do stunts with my gun.*
He dressed me like a pickle,
His favorite bastard son.
Tho' I had no money,
He was happy as could be;
In my coat of OD color,*
He had his way with me.
He taught me to stop blood
And how not to swoon.
I could even bandage up a sucking chest wound.
Tho' I had no money,
He was happy as could be;
In my coat of OD color,
He had his way with me.
He gave me two pairs of boots
And a pair of black shoes;
He kept me really busy,
So I couldn't sing the blues.

He gave me green underwear
And pairs of socks to match.
He even gave me a Screaming Eagle Patch.
I was justa poor boy,
From the hills of Tennessee;
He flew me across the ocean,
For all the Cong to see;
To continue my education in Rice Paddy U.
Do you have an Uncle who'd do that much for you?
In my coat of OD color that my Uncle gave to me,
I was warm and dry as a monsoon could be.
Tho' I had no money that didn't bother him none;
He gave me lots of ammo for my plastic gun.*
He never sewed a stitch that son of a bitch,
But he gave that thing to me;
I still have it back home,
In the hills of Tennessee.
More than forty summers
Have all come and gone.
Sometimes in the winter,
I still have it on;
Tho' it's old and faded,
I still wear it proudly;
The coat of OD color
That my Uncle gave to me.

* OD color – olive drab Uncle came – drafted 1st Dec. 1970
* gun – manual of arms
* plastic gun – M-16 had plastic parts

THE RE – UP

I was all in – the die was cast;
I must be wise so I would last.
We were given batteries of tests;
On all of them I did my best,
To give myself maximum flexibility,
To avoid armor, artillery and infantry.
The most dangerous were the combat arms,
Presenting booby traps and various other harms,
Like ambushes, bad food, and jungle rot.
I must find a "safe" comfortable spot,
One commensurate with my education;
Build my time and serve my nation.
To REMF hood* I must aspire;
Avoid the jungle muck and mire.
I disliked the Army you can be sure,
But I re-upped for another year,
For a most interesting military occupation;
One suited completely to my fascination,
With optics, images and photography.
A photo interpreter I'd surely be.
They said I had a high GT* score;
I was qualified and a little more.
Basic was not too hard nor a breeze;
We did our best just not to freeze.
I had the third highest PT* score,
Which left me proud, tired and sore.

* REMF – rear echelon (behind the lines M*****F****R)
* GT – general intelligence
* PT – physical training

Use this souvenir from Fort Holabird to become a trigonometry whiz. My astronomy students at The University of Tennessee liked this.

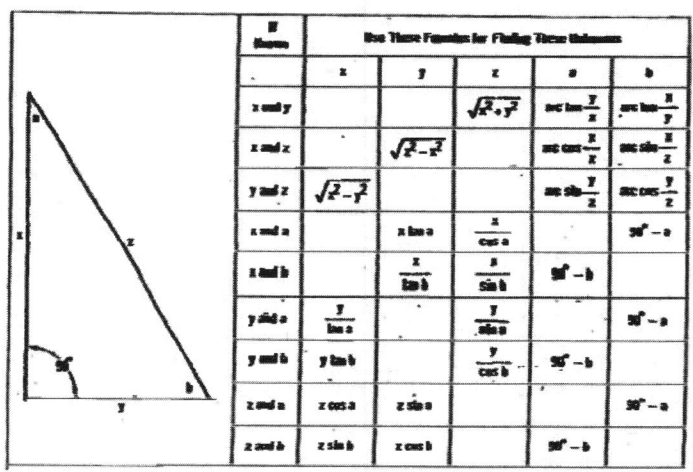

If shown	Use These Formulas for Finding These Unknowns				
	x	y	z	a	b
x and y			$\sqrt{x^2+y^2}$	$\arctan\frac{y}{x}$	$\arctan\frac{x}{y}$
x and z		$\sqrt{z^2-x^2}$		$\arccos\frac{x}{z}$	$\arcsin\frac{x}{z}$
y and z	$\sqrt{z^2-y^2}$			$\arcsin\frac{y}{z}$	$\arccos\frac{y}{z}$
x and a		$x\tan a$	$\frac{x}{\cos a}$		$90°-a$
x and b		$\frac{x}{\tan b}$	$\frac{x}{\sin b}$	$90°-b$	
y and a	$\frac{y}{\tan a}$		$\frac{y}{\sin a}$		$90°-a$
y and b	$y\tan b$		$\frac{y}{\cos b}$	$90°-b$	
z and a	$z\cos a$	$z\sin a$			$90°-a$
z and b	$z\sin b$	$z\cos b$		$90°-b$	

Basic Trigonometric Functions in a Right Triangle

The photo interpreter's

5   S's

1. Shape
2. Size
3. Shadows
4. Shade (tonality)
5. Surroundings

These were essential to identifying objects on aerial photos.

FORT HOLABIRD

At Fort Holabird I enjoyed myself;
It was more like school than anything else.
From 8 to 5 in Baltimore,
Interesting topics we did explore:
Map reading from maps and aerial photography,
Making mosaics and photogrammetry;*
Comporting well with my beloved astronomy
And solving the riddle of Soviet ID.*
We studied aerial photography from WWII
And much later stuff from the Vietnam zoo.
I bit my tongue and by fear was groped;
No stereo vision for me in the stereoscope;
It was a requirement hard and fast.
No stereo vision* and I couldn't last.
For this I'd taken another year;
To be in IPW* was my fear.
Before I could be counted home free,
Must pass a test in Soviet ID.*
I was told by an old NCO*,
You can't pass without stereo.
Out of 200 I scored 183,
Filling my soul with grateful glee.
It was the highest score don't you know;
I said nothing more about my stereo.
The image interpretation class was small,
Only 15 of us there were in all.

All of us had a college degree,
Except for two or was it three?
My chosen military occupation
Brought a satisfying sense of elation,
For the extra year I'd taken.
Never at work was there a dull day;
We were experts with something to say.
Immediately upon our graduation,
Our orders we received with trepidation.
Two for Korea and three for Germany;
Nine went to Vietnam along with me.

* photogrammetry – measuring objects on aerial photos
* Soviet ID – identifying Soviet tanks, guns, radar, missiles, etc. On aerial photography.
* Stereo vision – the ability to see objects in 3 dimensions on Aerial photography using a stereoscope
* IPW – Interrogation Prisoners of War
* NCO – Non commissioned officer

Chapter 2: Settling In 1971

In Vietnam

Verses (poems) 7 - 10

7. Trivia Night

8. Ancient Occupations

9. Airborne Cook

10. The Fourth of July in Camp Eagle

Gleanings from the latrine walls of the 90th Replacement in Long Binh:

Fighting for peace is like fornicating for chastity.

If God had meant for man to be in the Army, he would've been born with a green, baggy skin.

TRIVIA NIGHT

Waiting to be processed at Long Binh,
I realized the terrible mess I was in;
Never mind a bullet jagged or neat;
I might just die from the summer heat.
For several days I must sweat and wait,
'Til told by the posting of my in-country fate.
I tried to avoid the direct tropic sun;
Picking up butts was not much fun.
Hell fire, I didn't even smoke;
This must be a sadistic joke.
She brought some relief but not much joy;
It was easy to see she was no boy;
She was a Doughnut Dolly from the Red Cross,
A spirited filly not a plow hoss.
And though the place was hot as hell,
She was paid so very well.
A bringer of trivial fact and fun;
A half-baked blond in the tropic sun,
With a hint of a freckle here and there;
She had light blue eyes and light blond hair,
A round-eyed woman who'd merit a stare.
The whole thing was a rigged conspiracy;
Trivia chosen by Urania, the muse of astronomy.
Who was the first to measure the earth's size?
If you get it right, you get a prize.
No other hand shot up but mine;
Eratosthenes, I said feeling fine.

Who was first to propose a heliocentric cosmos?
No one would get this she surely supposed.
Again, no other hand in the air but mine;
Aristarchus, I said feeling fine.
Soon I got stares quizzical and queer;
Like man, what the hell are you doing here?
I thought the same for the rest of the year.
Dolly chose various other categories,
To give away goodies and esteemed glories.
I won not all but more than I could carry;
So I gave most away to Tom, Dick and Harry.
Not much room for candy, stationery and shaving cream;
The duffle bag was full of stuff dyed green.
At all my loot I took one long last look;
Then stuffed it beside my astronomy book.
Playing trivia was fun and fascination;
I knew the value of my college education.
It came to pass on the fourth day;
I was posted and soon away.
Was I blessed or was I cursed?
Away to Phu Bai with the 101st.

ANCIENT OCCUPATIONS

I ruv you beaucoup;*
You ruv me ti-ti.*
You give me bay-bee;
I give you VEE-DEE.
You give me mon-ey;
I be your hon-ey;
You souvenir* me 1000p*
In pidgin English she said to me.
Milhaus* came up on the double quick
And bugged her quarters subtle and slick.
I had no regrets for beds unmade,
Nor my gift of foreign aid.

* beaucoup – much
* ti –ti – little
* Milhaus – Tricky Dick's middle name
* souvenir – give me
* 1000 piasters or $2.38 US

This incident never happened personally to me as written. The
first six verses were the sing-song anthem of the Saigon
working girls.

The following perverse verse is a reflection of how it feels to be bossed by people who have made a career of being subpar. It is an allegory of the relationship between lifers and draftees.

AIRBORNE COOK

I knew a man whom reason never forsook;
He was clever as hell this airborne cook.
I've known PHDs from MIT and doctors of the law,
But they weren't nearly as bright,
And they couldn't hold a light,
To the man from Arkansas.
"Nixon was born of a virgin", he said,
As he fingered my pone of cold cornbread.
When I'd ask for eggs not raw,
He'd talk about his hogs in Arkansas.
I'm not trying to be explicit or crude,
But when you weren't looking,
There'd be stuff in your food.
Under a gook sun all parched and dry,
He'd taper* you off on dingleberry* pie.

* Taper you off – give as a dessert
* Dingleberry - crap

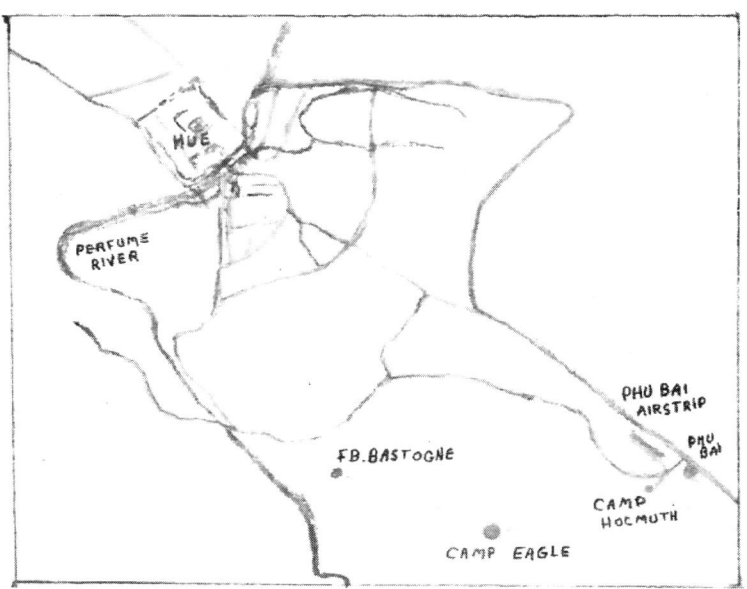

RF 1: 100,000   ├───┤ 1 MILE

I served a total of six months near HUE
in I Corps. Five months were spent in
Camp Hocmuth in Phu Bai and one
month in Camp Eagle. Fire Support
Base Bastogne saved our bacon.

THE FOURTH OF JULY IN CAMP EAGLE

Soldiers on the berm line began their celebration;
Two years and a half 'til my emancipation,
From my role as conscript soldier boy;
To shed my costume o' what a joy!
It was the 4th of July of '71;
My ordeal in Nam had just begun.
Surely as Darwin wrote *On the Origin of Species,*
The whole damned country reeked of urine and feces.
The sun rose red through a black pall of smoke;
Diesel in barrels was burning our shit;
A sight and smell I'll never forget.
Those not there may think it a joke;
It burned my nose and eyes;
Nothing Sam did could be a surprise.
This description is both accurate and crude;
It did not, however, improve the taste of our food.
Drinking all the water I could find,
I was melting not quite out of my mind.
A dark, foul mood came over me you know;
I longed to see a deep blanket of snow;
To feel the cold tingle of fingers and toes.
The spec 4 clerk let out a cry,
Assaulting my ears but not my eye.
You have a GT* score of 135;
You could've gone to OCS* - that ain't no jive.
My mood became so much darker still;
Sam, that bastard, I wanted to kill.

No opportunity was given for my choice;
He commanded me enlisted with raucous voice.
Sam was my worst enemy;
I would do nothing extra for free,
Unless it reflected great credit on me.
I loved my country but not my government,
Angered by the fool's errand on which I was sent.
I would demonstrate sham and skate;
Do my necessary duty and not hesitate.
To dissent was mutiny and treason;
I'd outflank that bastard any season.
I would never ever get caught
Doing things that I shouldn't ought.
Never busted or an article 15;
Nothing but a few gigs for my uniform.
Sam made me eschew harm,
Often feeling very mean.
Sam that rich, mean old pervert,
Always caused me extra hurt.

* GT – General Intelligence
* OCS – Officers Candidate School

Chapter 3: Phu Bai Adventures

Phu Bai, RVN, Republic of Vietnam

Verses (poems) 11 – 20

Big Al Fuerst and the author in July of '96

Laughing at my every wisecrack,

Forever not failing he had my back.

BIG AL FUERST

Together we made quite a team;
Cohorts riding on the same beam.
He was Dean Martin and I Jerry Lewis,
Banded together so Sam couldn't screw us.
Laughing at my every wisecrack,
Forever not failing he had my back.
Cool and collected under pressure,
He dispatched the enemy at his leisure.
We were Siamese twins from another mother;
Big Al to me was just like a brother;
We both had eschewed the infantry,
Rather choosing photographic imagery.
Bubbling over with enthusiasm and knowledge,
A graduate of Vienna and St. Leo's College,
Not the smartest man in the world or nation,
Only 13th or 14th by my precise estimation.
We don't see eye to eye politically;
But he is a half foot taller than me.
We agree to disagree;
Al is himself and I am me.
Concussion doesn't help the memory.
Some things were funny and some were rotten;
He recalls things that I've long forgotten.
At Camp Eagle sappers* were between guard posts,
Seeking to deliver what would damage most;

Blow up the choppers, ammo, and fuel,
Shoot up any stray early morning fool.
None of this was ever to be.
Al broke it all up with artillery,
Clearing our front and shell shocking me.
He saved our lives twice in 36 hours;
We lived to see a dead viper in the showers.
Faithful to his wife his stateside honey,
On Vietnamese liaisons he spent no money.
A career man he was in a word,
Not a dull Army lifer bird.
He was a peace maker and compromiser;
Quietly he made other folk wiser.
Negotiating without malice or fear;
In people skills he was without peer.
His expertise was his true wealth;
He thought more of others than himself.
My good friend still I'll have to say;
I wish him well each and every day.

* Sappers – Soldiers with explosive satchel charges

CLASS REUNION

In the mess hall in Phu Bai,
A familiar stranger passed me by;
He turned, came and sat down
And was newly arrived in town;
Attached to the Artillery across the street,
Assembled now our breakfast to eat;
Our reunion was amazing after all;
We couldn't refuse the draft board's call.
We were college grads and privates too,
Inmates in the Camp Hockmuth zoo.
Scarcely a year and a half before,
We stood outside the very same door,
Back in the world, Jefferson City, Tennessee;
We were part of the class of 1970.
Off campus roommates we had been,
'Til the last big draft sucked us in.
I found a rock in my eggs I thought,
But my best guess was all for naught;
It turned out to be I must say in truth,
A large filling from a molar tooth.
After a few weeks I saw him no more,
But he still lives somewhere on the shore,
In old Virginia where he was born,
Never to become a star of porn,
But a successful member of the Virginia bar,
Spreading his services near and far.

HANOI HANNAH

At a combat base in Phu Bai,
We closely scanned the humid sky,
With my homemade telescope,
Taking in all the celestial dope;
Showing Big Al the lunar features,
Craters, mountains but no moon creatures.
Perched on top of a five-ton van,
We scanned the skies of that Asian land.
The sky was never very clear or dark;
Flares lit up like lights in a park.
With my shortwave just for a lark,
We listened in the growing dark.
She sounded like a California chick;
You boys are tired and so homesick.
This is not your war she said;
Why should you die? Your cause is dead.
We will be here when you're gone.
Go ahead and carry on;
Jody has your girl and gone.
Come on over to our side;
Keep your dignity and your pride.
Many girls in beautiful Hanoi want to marry an American boy;
Throw down your guns and chieu hoi.*
She said it true and direct,
Nixon is a lying sockcucker, or profound words to that affect.
Said I to Big Al, my best pal, she is a Democrat just like me.
Folks really like Dick in Tennessee.

Don't be a fool she firmly said;
People forget you when you're dead.
Until tomorrow I'll have to say,
Be careful and have a nice day.
Watch out for snakes in the high jungle grass;
There may be an ambush in the Hi Ban Pass.
Sleep well and good nighty night;
For now, Phu Bai is all right!

* chieu hoi – defect to our side

Chief Warrant Officer 3

CW3

Insignia on Hat

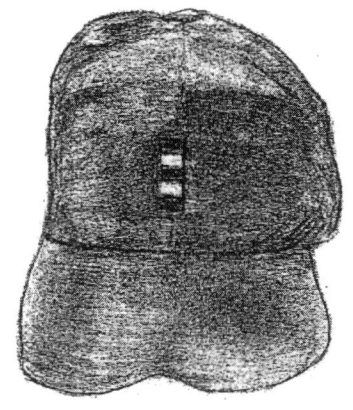

RECON MAN SLEEPY STAN

He was clean shaven and smelled like Old Spice;
For a damned yankee he was very nice.
He had a slight limp, old, tired and sore;
A bonified veteran of the Army Air Corps.
He'd been doing this since World War II;
For him a most natural thing to do.
He'd been in a Bird Dog over France and Germany,
An old Warrant Officer – a CW* three.
I don't know if he knew Jesus,
But I never heard him cuss;
He kept to himself – I never heard him fuss.
I was tired just getting off my twelve hour shift;
To the airstrip we must go;
Most surely, dude, you know that I was miffed.
Only two more months and he'd go home,
Back to Elmira and sit upon his throne.
He'd been a man of valor and showed a lota pluck,
As he stowed his gear away and climbed into the truck.
On the way to the airstrip he couldn't doze or sleep;
The ride was rough much rougher than a Jeep.
I popped the clutch and raked a lota gears;
That's what happens, dude, when you're not a volunteer;
White knuckled he clung to his seat and dash;
I got my revenge, poor, white mountain trash.
Like a sailor in a storm about to capsize,
I saw the fear deep inside that old man's eyes.

Have you been driving long? He weakly asked of me.
I started driving on the farm along about '53;
It wasn't really my fault I looked at him and said,
But for the grace of God I'd killed my Daddy dead;
He was hooking up the tractor when my foot slipped the clutch.
After that he said that he never liked me much.
We were hungry for awhile and sold off half the farm;
It cost a lot of money to patch his leg and arm.
He's still kinda crippled back in Tennessee;
There's no way in hell, sir, he'd ever ride with me.
As we jostled and swerved along the way,
I was having a most blessed, vengeful day.
He'd been shot at over Germany and crash landed in France;
But on the way to the airstrip did he really crap his pants?
He had two guardian angels and one Keebler Elf,
If he had a Saint Christopher's he never crossed himself.
He was feeling better at the airstrip you could tell;
Over the DMZ* he'd be shot at – things were going swell.
Officers were in charge and some of them were smart;
You've got to educate them right from the start;
Break them from suckin'aigs* as we say in Tennessee;
There was no way in hell, sir, they'd ever ride with me.

* CW3 – Chief Warrant Officer ranking above enlisted grades
        but below commissioned officers
* DMZ – demilitarized zone
* Suckin' aigs – Sucking eggs, a Southernism denoting any
        offensive habit

Cessna O-1 Bird Dog

THE BIRD DOG JOY RIDE

I did it for my ego and not for my id;
Perhaps the dumbest thing that I ever did.
Mike took me to the airstrip in downtown Phu Bai,
I was a volunteer and not on orders to fly.
On the Ben Hai River northwest of Hue,*
We sought out the enemy that mid August day,
The captain pilot gave me a brown paper bag and a grin;
Just in case you're airsick catch your breakfast here within.
She was a veteran of 3 wars well suited for the job,
Flying low and level true as a brass plumb bob.
Built for observation with lots of plexiglass;
You could see movement in the tall elephant grass.
The Bird Dog was a two seater with two sets of controls;
He was fond of many wig-wags and a few barrel rolls.
Thinking it necessary for my fitness test,
To make me puke he did his dead level best.
In all this no reward was ever found;
Barely, just barely, I kept it all down.
The pilot spotted in a clearing a cache sight;
He swung around to line up the hooch just right.
There was a whoosh as the rocket took flight;
Right of the hooch he had greatly missed.
Once more he tried diving, spinning from above;
I closed my eyes cutting off the spinning mist.
Only 15 meters much closer than before;
A closer miss but still a miss,

Setting the grass asmoking and afire;
His homemade sight was somewhat a liar.
There was a MIG nearby he said in a steady mood.
The prophecy on the wall said that we were really screwed.
He had good news – the best ever yet;
The MIG was just downed by a Navy jet.
He was on the radio – we didn't have a phone,
Calling in a mission from Fire Base Bastogne
To take care of the cache site;
The Arty Boys could do it up right.
Not wanting to be shot down by our artillery,
From the air space we were forced to flee.
On the way back to Phu Bai, it was really neat,
He let me fly the Bird Dog from my back seat.
To fly ever again I had no such desire;
I would not be the bait to draw enemy fire.
Ten days later that Bird Dog pilot was no more,
Along with my hooch mate* who hailed from Baltimore.
I did it for my ego and not for my id;
Perhaps the dumbest thing that I ever did.

* Hue – pronounced Whey
* hooch mate – lived beside me in our plywood quarters

BURNING BIRD DOG

A bright young man in the prime of life,
With two young sons and a beautiful wife;
Never to return to Baltimore
Or walk the strands of the Eastern Shore.
The best volleyballer in Detachment A,
Off the net the ball he could play.
In the Nam it was cool to fly;
A lofty position, a natural high.
There was a bad omen in the sky;
The ruddy God of War was in opposition,*
To demand more sacrifice shades of perdition.
With my Norton's* well in hand,
I taught him the stars in that tortured land.
He was the Backseat in a Bird Dog *;
An aerial observer through clouds and fog.
High ship, low ship over the DMZ*;
He fought to make others free.
That day he was in the low ship,
When he made his final trip.
He was the bait for the NVA*
As he flew on that August day.
The trick was to draw fire;
So the high ship could aspire
To get a fix on their fire.
Killed on impact with the ground,
With a battalion of enemy all around.

And only 30 days to DEROS*;
Joined to the pantheon of heroes.
Back in base camp we heard the news;
It was deadly serious not a ruse.
After awhile the Bird Dog burned;
Soon enough it was the enemy's turn.
The Navy scrambled Crusader jets;
Crispy critters made you can bet.
Peace with honor* cost him his life;
Personal effects went to Julianne his wife.
Years later I visited the wall*;
His name was easily seen by all.
He got an extra hundred and ten*,
Just for his hazardous flying;
The extra pay needless to say,
Wasn't worth his own dying.

* Opposition – Mars was close to Earth
* Norton's – Norton's Star Atlas
* Bird Dog – two seat overwing plane with a top speed of about 100 mph
* DMZ – demilitarized zone between North and South Vietnam
* NVA - North Vietnamese Army
* DEROS – date expected to return from overseas
* Honor – Peace with honor, Nixon's policy of gradual withdrawal cost another 20,000 American War dead
* Wall – the U.S. memorial to American war dead
* Ten - $110 extra pay per month

Grumman OV-1 Mohawk

DOZER IN THE DMZ

There were shades of black and white,
Wrought in the humid jungle night.
Rumors of its existence did abound,
Till the infrared rendered found,
The invasion route upon the ground.
The triple jungle canopy,
Made by day so hard to see.
And so they worked day and night,
Southward to bring military might.
One night I did chance to see a bulldozer glowing hot and white,
Not safe from the all-seeing eye of the Mohawk* from Phu Bai.
There on frames of infrared,
Brought to me a sense of dread.
The prospect of being overrun,
Comported not my sense of fun;
I wanted to withdraw gracefully,
Not killed by hordes of infantry.
Much in the Army was naught but crap,
But by George I could read a map.
On the phone I called G-2 air*;
Gave them coordinates to the where.
A gunship to do it up right,
To kill them all that very night
Was sent by the Air Force;
Good work done as a matter of course.
In only about two hours time,

I went to the airstrip to find
The roll of film waiting for me;
To be processed so I could see;
The results of our combined endeavor,
 So precise and so very clever.
I took it all personally;
They were coming to kill me
 And the thinning brave company.
It was completely satisfying;
Tonight the enemy did all the dying.
I slept pleasantly the next day,
Knowing last night I'd earned my pay.
And for now, Phu Bai was alright.
The gunship had made quite a jumble;
A pile of junk there in the jungle.
Hand to hand we wouldn't fight,
Because we had got it right.

* Mohawk – the Army's multi-sensor Surveillance Aircraft
* G-2 – the division level military Intelligence Department
   coordinating air power.

THE PHU BAI NIGHT SHIFT

Not all my Army experiences were negative;
The Phu Bai night shift was the most positive.
My life is better now and forever;
It was a brain enhancer like a lever.
Working together the whole night through,
There was always little or nothing to do.
But when from Phu Bai the Mohawks* did fly,
Not much escaped their all-seeing eyes;
The night was scant cover or protection,
For hostiles headed in our direction.
We got recon imagery from infrared
And radar that caught them moving ahead.
We were the aerial night watch while others slept;
How many enemy were killed and their widows wept?
There were only the two of us;
No officers to watch, berate or cuss;
I must say to save my soul,
Most of our officers had better control.
Working so late we got another meal;
C-rations did not always appeal;
So we swapped tit for tat;
I'll give you this for that.
He was the habitual smoker
And I the perpetual joker.
My physics prof gave me a teacher's edition
That suited my duffle bag's stuffed condition.

All I wanted to know about astronomy
Was there in a 700 page text waiting for me.
On nights when there was nothing to do,
I did the problems and read the text through.
I still have that text home with me,
At Starcrest, my farm in Tennessee.
Many years later on the Knoxville hill,
A dream came true, my ultimate thrill.
I taught astronomy on that hallowed hill.
Much like Nashvillian Emerson Barnard*,
Self-taught my knowledge came slow and hard.
Comets bought Barnards's bride a house;
The Phu Bai night shift bought my spouse
An eight acre farm and a big house.
Enough of my self-centered pride;
Thank you, Lord, you did provide.
Memories of the Army are not all bad;
Thoughts of Phu Bai banish so many things sad.

* Barnard – 1857 – 1923 Tennessee astronomer who
  discovered 10 comets in a short period of time and used the
  prize money to build a new house.
* Mohawks – OV-1 Mohawk multisensory Army surveillance
  aircraft.

There's an old Tennessee Mountain Proverb that I just made up:

If'n hit haint mine, then hit must be urine.

Urine (yours or your one)

THE GOVERNMENT INSPECTOR

I never parachuted into Normandy;
But with 101st I made history.
Too many soldiers were becoming thugs,
Killing their pain with opioid drugs.
I gave not my full measure of devotion;
That first drug test caused quite a commotion.
Giving my live sample of pee
Was keeping my country strong and free.
A rotten-toothed sergeant from Tennessee
Was staring a hole in the middle of me.
He had a bemused halfwit grin,
Watching pee in the cup dribble in.
I liked not his jocular stare;
I was pissed just being there.
Just some more abject humiliation,
To futilely serve an ungrateful nation.
With ten milliliters of my very best,
I tested negative and passed the test.
No candy, medal, or even a sticker;
No beer, wine, or moonshine liquor.
The medical officer noted something amiss;
The Sarge was too much into our piss;
He was relieved and so then were we,
The salacious sergeant from Tennessee.

It was not a weapon of war or hate,

But a Red Delicious from Washington State.

FRAGGING THE CAPTAIN

Captain Martin Mercantile
Was never seen to crack a smile.
An artilleryman from upstate New York;
He stood at five and a half feet short.
A relic from the Korean War;
Advanced in his career not so far.
He took a negative shine to me
And liked not my twang from Tennessee,
Nor the way the things I said;
Nor my shiny spit-shined head.
Something there was stuck in his craw;
Was he sucker punched by his ma?
Something rotten his soul did vex;
Was he too cheap to pay for sex?
To provoke unnecessarily in a combat zone
Was a good way not to get back home.
He screwed with us night and day;
No refractory period and no foreplay.
So one day in the mess hall,
Me thought of a way to end it all.
I took my apple to my beloved captain,
A slightly enlarged version of Charlie Chaplin.
Less than a fortnight before,
Two officers were fragged at the mess hall door;
Dead lying in their pools of blood,
Mingling with the rain and mud.
From the mess hall to the big van,
I walked with the apple in hand.

In the van it caused quite a stir,
Cussing the captain and saying not sir.
Pulling an imaginary pin I tossed it in;
And cussing the captain yet once again.
Visions of no retirement danced in his head,
Fearing in the Nam he'd soon be dead.
Alas the apple grenade was a dud,
Landing on his desk with a thud.
It was not a weapon of war or hate,
But a Red Delicious from Washington State.
He had a mustache and close cropped hair,
But me thinks he needed clean underwear.
The pompous ass and strutting cock,
Became the company's laughing stock.
Enlisted men always gave him a salute,
Thinking all the while of the deadly fruit.
From the captain's wrath I wasn't insured;
Off to Camp Eagle I was transferred
To become the eyes of the eagle,
And the brains of the bird,
But the major had the final word.
Later I became a Tennessee teacher
And was never ordained a Baptist preacher.

Chapter 4: Camp Eagle 1971

The B-52 – Targeting Section

RVN (South Vietnam)

Verses (poems) 21 - 31

21. The Screaming Chicken Patch

22. The Gentle Reprimand

23. Smiling Papasan

24. A Nineteen Gun Salute

25. Special Oops Soldiers

26. Townsend Talks

27. Perimeter Sweep

28. Commandeering the Commandant's Commode

29. Tear Gassed

30. The 101st Airborne Psalm

31. Death and Taxes ARVN Style

THE SCREAMING CHICKEN PATCH

My first day on the Camp Eagle job,
With unpressed fatigues – a soldierly slob.
Sergeant Smith who was a most practical man,
Pressed four division patches into my hand,
Giving directions to me most imprecise;
He would send me away – a roll of the dice.
Off base a seamstress I must surely find;
Perhaps myself shot or step on a mine.
Smith returned almost exuding charm,
Happy to see the bird on my arm.
My, that was a trip so very quick.
Sarge, off base I never did went;
I stuck the patch on with rubber cement.
He must have thought me an insubordinate prick,
But I thought it a measure neat and slick.
He was not pleased I really must say,
But he gave me off the rest of the day.
As I was going out he was coming in,
The biggest Vietnamese ever – General Big Minh.
The memory of it still makes me smile;
How many Mongolians in the family wood pile?
She was conversant and trying to please;
There was no eagle for the Vietnamese.
Chicken-man soldier numbah one she said,
Engendering thoughts in my thick blockhead.
I had one extra Screaming Eagle patch;
In truth I never wanted it to match.

A most amazing sight to see,
A seamstress so expert in embroidery.
The eagle became a fighting gamecock,
Like a chicken you cook in a crock.
The bird had a wattle and a comb;
Too bad I never got it back home.
The officers never saw it as about I went;
It was put on neatly with rubber cement.
A proud member of the chairborne infantry;
A private joke between Big Al and me.

Richard M. Nixon 37th President of the United States

1969 – 1974

was a crook and much more. Immensely popular with the public, he
was re-elected with over 70% of the popular vote. He was detested
only slightly less than LBJ by the draftees.

A GENTLE REPRIMAND

I had the day shift; Al had the night;*
We worked together to get it all right.
We didn't do it alone of course;
We had the help of the US Air Force.
When 50 tons of bombs fall from the sky,
It was paramount the right people die.
Too hot that December day,
Chained to the lighttable* I did stay.
I was feeling a bit too perverse;
Things could have been so very much worse.
The officers standing around stood their ground,
Sorely amazed at some things I'd found.
There was a patch of pot there in the jungle,
And a camouflage job that Nguyen* did bungle.
How it was I did what I do;
They had not the ghost of a clue.
Rather I had a cold Budweiser;
Than another worthless supervisor.
While my day so slowly passed,
They smoked and joked and played grabass.
Reading magazines and munching fruit,
Always giving me someone to salute.
Not so good as Stonewall Jackson,
Suffering constipation from chronic inaction.
In a land of smoke and fog,
Useless as tits on a big boar hog.

I drew up a target on the Rung-Rung Valley,
A hit job better suited to Lieutenant Calley.*
To turn the valley into a lunarscape,
Was tantamount to murder and rape.
Not so criminal as murder or incest,
The following ditty I sang in protest.

(To the tune of "Jesus Loves All the Children")

NIXON BOMBS ALL THE CHILDREN

Nixon bombs all the children,
All the children of the world;
Red and yellow, black or white,
Just as long as they can't write.
To their congressmen in Washington, D.C.;
Nixon bombs all the children,
All the children of the world;
When they bow their heads to pray,
He will blow their shit away.
Nixon bombs all the children of the world.

Early the very next day,
A butterbar* came to say:
O' holy crap, O' holy cow,
The major will see you in his office now.
Major Hicksford of Hicksville, North Carolina,
Of the officer corps, none could be finer,

With curly red hair but no red nose,
A very large man in very large clothes.
By the oak leaf he must be smart;
But Lordy how he could belch and fart,
Blowing smoke from his foul cigar;
Broadcasting orders both near and far.
Private Noland to me he said,
As though I had not a thought in my head,
Do you know what inertia* is?
Very proud to show off my knowledge;
Yes, sir, I had physics in college.
We need to get more work done around here;
I hope I make myself perfectly clear.
Like a clown or a big rock star,
He waved me off with his cigar.
Had he been Jesus and I a whore,
Surely to me he would implore.
Get thee hence thou unclean bitch;
Go and sing no more.
The day started out so very sucky;
All in all I got off so lucky.
Back to the lighttable I did go,
Taking my time but not too slow.
Grateful but never losing face,
Working at my same old pace;
Carefully reading out the imagery;
After all they depended on me.

* Big Al – Albert Fuerst – my best friend. Recipient of a Bronze Star for calling in artillery on our own position.
*Lighttable – lit the duo-positive film from behind to make image interpretation possible (think black and white transparency).
*Nguyen – very common Vietnamese name.
*Butterbar – 2nd Lt.
*Inertia – resistance to change, Newton's first law
*Calley – Scapegoat convicted of the My Lai massacre. Got 20 years in prison – pardoned by President Carter.

Was he a nocturnal VC

Or an angel from heaven?

With a conical hat and staff in hand,

A most accomplished professional man.

SMILING PAPASAN

The sergeant had a job for me,
Or so he said with muffled glee;
The final link in the food chain,
The stench of which caused mental pain.
Not caring that I was sorely pissed,
Nor minding that I'd never re-enlist.
Sarge explained in extended detail,
To use enough diesel or I would fail;
Thinking, perhaps, I hadn't sufficient education
To pull off such a complex operation.

OR

I could pay off papasan
And watch him have all the fun.
The latter option suited just fine,
Getting mine arse out of a bind.
Standing at about four eleven
Was he a nocturnal VC
Or an angel from heaven?
With a conical hat and staff in hand,
A most accomplished professional man.
We bowed slightly to each other;
In the cause he became a brother.
I paid him off in MPC;*
He became a great fan of me.
Giving him twice the going rate.

Gladly, I did not ever hesitate.
It was only a dollar to me;
For him a treasure for eternity.
How old he was I couldn't really tell,
A long life of strife and constant hell.
Not as well appointed as Howard Hughes,
He wore rubber tires for his sandal shoes,
Being the last drop of the trickle down.
Wearing a smile and not a frown;
Had he a rep throughout the town?
As poor as the rich Vietnamese dirt,
He'd long suffered a life of hurt.
First the French and the Japanese,
And now the fat Americans
He strove hard to please.
Wiry he was and incredibly strong,
Dragging half barrels of crap along.
I admired his strong dexterity,
Not getting a drop on himself or me.
When three half barrels were in place,
He proceeded along with measured pace.
From a secret family recipe,
He added fuel to all the three.
Then with a piece of paper and a Bic,
The half barrels ignited hot and quick.
Like a Grand Master of Kung Fu,
He constantly stirred the burning doo.
He couldn't go home after a year;
His roots and life were always here.

God bless thee, grandfatherly gook,
For burning all of the company's poop.
In all thy fine resplendent glory,
Thou wert the Commandant of the Crap Crematory.

* MPC – Military Payment Certificate

105 mm Howitzer in action

Private Noland taking cover

Incoming was on the way;
I wanted to live another day.
'twas not a time for excessive mirth;
Behind the bunker I hugged the earth.

A NINETEEN GUN SALUTE

'twas the night before,
The night before Christmas
And all through the 'Nam
Were plenty of NVA* and Viet Cong.*
Little ol' me and Big Al Fuerst,
My bestest pal in 101st
Were guarding Camp Eagle
On a wet winter's night.
At half past 3 with a leaden sky,
Behind the bunker I got shuteye.
Passing our front were eight NVA.
Was it to be a really bad day?
He'd rather be home eating ham
Than guarding a berm in Viet Nam.
To live another day was his desire,
But the M-60 wouldn't fire.
Big Al thought to play asleep,
As past the NVA did creep.
When they faded from sight,
He set about to make things right,
Giving the Div Arty boys something to do;
They had coordinates the boys at Bastogne;
We were supported and not alone.
Think me not a lowlife cur,
If I employ a racial slur.
Saith Big Al — not a direct quote:
Wake up Garry or it's all she wrote.

Wake up and piss;
The world's on fire!
Wake up Garry!
There're gooks in the wire!
Incoming was on the way;
I wanted to live another day.
'twas not a time for excessive mirth;
Behind the bunker I hugged the earth.
The first round hit 25 meters away;
My brain switched off – no time to pray.
It's a fact I won't dispute;
My guardian angel not a drunken brute,
Nor AWOL in a house of ill repute.
I kept my life and private parts,
Thanks to Big Al and his timely smarts.
No paper work – no Purple Heart.
There was no blood for me;
Only irritability and PTSD.*
The fire was adjusted 40 meters out;
The final result was never in doubt.
Another 18 rounds tore the sky asunder,
Sounding like freight trains and claps of thunder.
At first light in early morn,
The ground was pocked, bloody and torn.
Only bits and pieces were ever found,
On that dark and soggy ground.
Big Al was no kinda clunker,
Safe inside that concrete bunker;
A bronze star was his just reward.
My hearing was damaged and hard.

We got to live another day,
But not so with the NVA.

* NVA – North Vietnamese Army
* Viet Cong – irregular local communist troops
* PTSD – Post Traumatic Stress Disorder
  Known in WWI as Shell Shock and WWII and Korea as Battle
  Fatigue

B-52 Bomber

Oops! I targeted Camp Eagle
due to a traumatic concussion.
Artillery fire helps not the higher
cognitive functions.
Fortunately, Al Fuerst caught the mistake.

SPECIAL OOPS SOLDIERS

I seek neither shame nor glory;
What I relate is a true story.
I was shell-shocked with no rest;
Thirty plus hours I'd done my best.
Waking me to go back to work,
The sergeant was not a malignant jerk;
Just following orders like everyone.
It could well have been our last sun;
Another horrid day in infamy;
The blame not clear for history.
Big Al had called in the artillery;
Right on top of him and me.
I hugged the earth and was not dead,
My brain bouncing around inside my head.
Later that day,
As I worked away;
To target an infiltration route,
On the border of Laos and Nam no doubt.
Big Al, the night shift came in;
Sleepily I stroked my chin.
I'm not sure about the grid designator;
After I left he checked it out later.
What he saw was pure hell not heck;
The hair raised on the back of his neck.
X-ray Delta* is what I'd used;
I had it wrong being confused.

Yankee Charlie was sorely needed;
A distinction that I hadn't heeded.
X-ray Delta would put the arc light,
On top of Camp Eagle – not too bright.
It would've vaporized me and Big Al Fuerst,
And the 3rd Brigade of the 101st.
Big Al ran hard to the DTOC*;
Trying not to die from the shock.
They were loading bombs in Thailand,
To take care of the problem at hand.
The Air Force lieutenant hadn't done his job;
That was work becoming an enlisted slob.
Why should he work tonight?
We had always had it right.
The Air Force would've bombed coordinates unchecked;
And the albatross would hang from around his neck.
Christmas would have been a sad day;
With hundreds or thousands blown away.
Big Al deserved another medal or two;
He knew how and just what to do.
Christmas Bob Hope had a place to go;
Just why that was he'd never know.
It just wasn't our time to go;
Thanks to Big Al who made it so.
A self-inflicted Dien Bien Phu*
Would have saddened Nixon too.

*X-ray Delta – grid designator that shifted the target 62 miles too far to the east.

* DTOC –Division Tactical Operations Center

* Dien Bien Phu – place where French paratroopers were wiped out by General Giap in 1954

TOWNSEND TALKS

The division bulletin board said, Townsend Talks;
A green weenie in the guise of a banana;
Slightly more believeable than Hanoi Hannah.
It was propaganda plain and simple,
Festering in my brain a rebellious pimple.
On his shoulders he wore three stars;
Earned on the battlefield not in bars.
He was a paratrooper in Normandy,
Deserving of respect from others and me.
His BS sought to twist and spin,
Making it seem we all would win.
Would the government ever lie to us?
Don't get me started or I'll rant and cuss.
Something he said struck me as queer;
If Vietnamization was working,
Then why ever were we here?
Seeking a fourth star he followed the party line;
What I expected with me it was fine.*
I wanted him not to think us all stupid;
He, a lieutenant general, not a cohort of cupid.
On the bulletin board of division headquarters,
I made with my sharpie just for starters,
Some comments to assist the CG*,
With his truth telling deficiency.
The headliner stated Townsend Talks;
With my pen I scribed Eagles Scream, pigs oink, dogs bark, and
chickens squawk.

Jackasses bray and Townsend Talks.
Early next morning without fanfare or warning,
I confessed straightway to Big Al,
My confederate and yankee pal.
Al was looking at the bulletin board,
Approached by a light colonel surely bored.
Fuerst, he said sounding pissed,
I bet you know who did this.
Mine arse would've been in a sling,
But Big Al did his fibbing thing.
No, sir, answered he, with a floppy grin.
I have not even the slightest clue;
Whoever did has a loose screw!
That was not the end of the story;
Copycats inspired reflected glory.
Bulletin boards all over the place,
Sprouted graffiti – what a disgrace!
Nobody cared so very much anymore;
They were bound back to the American shore.
No more patrolling, guard duty or body bags,
Shedding their Army costumes for civy rags.

* Fine – He wanted to be politically correct not to damage his
  chances for promotion.
* CG – commanding general

Why did you shoot that big cobra snake?

Perturbed Al queried the point man Jake.

PERIMETER SWEEP

Trying to stay alive in that torrid nation;
Another wonderful day of his Asian vacation.
By the clock it was time for his daily sleep;
He had to give it up for a perimeter sweep.
Seek and ye shall surely find
Spider holes, booby traps and buried mines.
Colonel Whiney to Big Al said,
Don't get yourself or the others dead;
Piles of paper work we surely dread.
Fuerst, you dumb sonofabitch , go;
You're in charge make it so.
You're not an officer and you're not God;
You're a spec 4 in charge of the squad.
Al chose the rest of the crew;
They hated him for what he did do.
Just being there was grief beyond compare;
Nothing in life or war that's fair.
They were well equipped without a doubt.
Heavy gear never makes a Pentecostal shout.
As a matter of protocol,
In at certain check points they'd call.
At the second check point things were ok;
Perhaps they were having a very rice day.
Advance slowly looking for thin trip wires;
Searching the tree line for dinky outliers.
Naturally the point man Jake Purvis,

Had a right to be sullen and nervous.
There were no atheists in rice paddies,
'Cause on the draft board served their daddies.
He was a Pentecostal from Arkansas,
Appreciating not all the paysage* he saw.
Not a snake handler but a bench hopper*;
In his ebullience was stuffed a stopper.
Big Al was bringing up the rear,
Scanning vistas both far and near.
It was very serious and not a trifle;
The air was rent by an automatic rifle.
The squad hit the rice paddy deck,
Mucking up their faces and their necks.
Big Al was in a pissed off condition.
Why did you give away our position?
Why did you shoot that big cobra snake?
Perturbed Al queried the point man Jake.
Standing calmly by a rice paddy dike,
Replied he – no time for an air strike,
I hope you'll surely understand;
I'm not a French kissin' cobra man!
They beat a hasty retreat being compromised;
At this no one should ever be surprised.
But for the snake, all fared well;
It made a neat story for all to tell.
Jake, the snake, Purvis was a celebrity,
Quaffing beers that he got for free.
He made it back home to Arkansas
To sit on the porch with Maw and Paw.

In retrospect Al thought it amusing;
The Army was his sleep abusing.
Colonel Whiney even had good news;
No more sweeps for the MI* dudes.

*Paysage – French for countryside
*Bench hopper – worshiper in an ecstatic state jumping up on a
 church pew to preach, testify, etc.
*MI – Military Intelligence

Rank

Has

Its

Privileges

The general had the rank

and Al took the privilege.

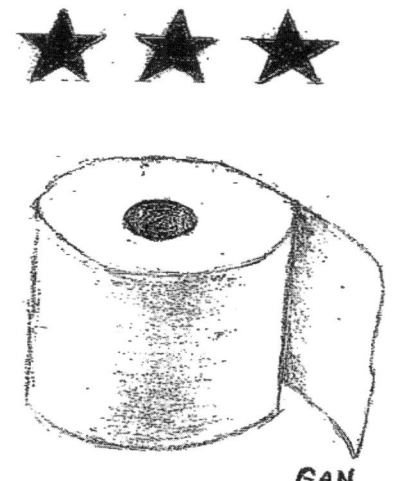

GAN

COMMANDEERING THE COMMANDANT'S COMMODE

Generals were asleep at night as a rule;
Al was desperate not a reckless fool.
Sometime soon after the midnight mess,
The call of nature left him in distress.
The enlisted latrine was crowded and stinky;
He moved from shadow to shadow like a slinky,
'Til he was in the commandant's holy temple;
An act of defiance risky and simple.
Like a peasant in the halls of the king,
He did his grand bowel movement thing.
Like a sneaky dog on his master's bed,
The adrenaline rush went to his head;
So much fun and yet quite alarming;
The clandestine act was habit forming.
A Polaroid he wanted for posterity,
A nice color photo for all to see.
In the wood paneled walls there was no crack;
The glorious immortals had a rack,
For magazines and shelves for knickknacks.
There was no marble on the bathroom floor,
But there was a sturdy lock on the door.
There were civilian toilet paper, lights and a fan;
Al was a fortunate, happy, commodious man.
Word got back via the old grapeviney;
Someone was grousing like old Colonel Whiney.
Lowlife people or persons unknown,
Had usurped the great man's throne.

TEAR GASSED

It was my last week at Camp Eagle,
For entertainment I was most eager;
Two days after Christmas in '71,
To the EM* Club I went for fun;
A ramshackle building by the berm line,
For the purposes intended it served just fine.
It was crowded and stinky the atmosphere;
I soaked it all up along with the beer.
It was a round-eyed Aussie affair;
The lead guitarist had long hair and a beard;
What soon happened I had never feared.
They were a really good band;
The boys gave them a really good hand.
All three girls were talented and sweet,
Tempting as a smokehouse hung with meat.
In fishnet hose and high heeled shoes,
They sang a lot of rock and a little bit of blues.
About half way through "Proud Mary",
We all left in a great hurry.
I heard a loud pop and saw black smoke;
All too soon we all began to choke.
Running and choking for a long way;
A rotten ending to a wretched day;
To the boys in the boonies a near paradise;
Just a few tears to cleanse out the eyes.
We all returned but never went in;
Seems they were multitasking in sin.

They had left their far away shores,
Seeking their fortunes as musical whores.
There was no need for me to longer stay;
I had all the fun I could stand that day.
Maybe better luck with the officer corps.

* EM – Enlisted Men's Club

101ST AIRBORNE PSALM

I will lift mine eyes unto the fire bases from whence cometh my support. He that were stoned in Caracas* suffereth not my foot to be moved nor his face to be lost in Asia. He maketh me to lie down in rice paddies and leadeth me beside the stinking waters. He restoreth the status quo. My cup runneth over with filth. Yea, though I walk through the Ashau Valley I shall fear every evil for his rod and general staff are comfortable. He prepareth a table before me in the presence of mine enemies. He igniteth their heads with oil*. There is a bomb in Gilead. He bombeth the dikes and smiteth the Gook even unto the fifth generation. Not one stone remaineth upon another and no green thing groweth. Surely he hath no goodness nor mercy as shone by the days of his life and I shall dwell in the Nam forever.

*Caracas — Nixon as Eisenhower's VP was stoned by
   protestors in Caracas
* Oil - napalm
* King Richard Nixon

Written to express my disappointment at being reassigned and not sent home with the 101st.

DEATH AND TAXES ARVN STYLE

Things were going from bad to worse,
With the steady withdrawal of the 101st.
The rapture had left Big Al behind,
Not a condition to which he was inclined;
Doing nothing to ease a troubled mind.
Being the best often has a downside;
On mission impossible you're sure to ride.
Clear thinking under pressure was his saving grace,
Checking mistakes in the war's ebb and pace;
He could often outflank or about-face.
Tested by fire in the tribulation,
He was there to save the ARVN* nation,
To keep I corps from being overrun;
Targeting arc lights* he was number 1.
Training our Vietnamese allies to use the B-52
Was a complicated dangerous thing to do;
There were always unintended consequences,
Trying to maintain the political fences.
One night some LRRPS* came in to see Al,
Pissed to the max and not his pal.
All the officers bailed out right away;
Would Al even see another day?
Finally the lieutenant made the sarge,
Who was very angry and very large,
Put his drawn pistol away.
Fuerst, you worthless son of a hound;
A friendly village is a hole in the ground.

The village was not targeted by the division;
Our Vietnamese allies came under suspicion.
They gave Al only a few days,
Holy hell they constantly raised;
He must correct the situation;
Friendly villages faced annihilation.
The ARVN were their own worst enemies;
Pacified villages were abused as they pleased,
Driving them into the arms of the North Vietnamese.
A contingent of ARVN would fly in,
Then the shakedown would begin;
They'd raise the national flag,
Soon to become a national rag,
Play on loudspeakers the national anthem,
Loot for taxes and ransack 'em,
Cuff around the elders of the village,
Rape at will and further pillage.
With such friends and allies as these,
Why worry about the North Vietnamese?
Al called the higher ups to get an angle,
Every one below the rank of arch angel.
The military hierarchy has hide bound logic,
Following the rules engenders things tragic.
For purely political reasons,
Death was never out of season.
Al soon developed a workable strategy;
Extra time he had none free.
The arc light could be in flight diverted,
For a target of higher priority,

An ingenious ruse you surely see.
Al always sought right to do his portion
And would not be part of the ARVN extortion.
Tacitly Colonel Whiney the division G-2*,
Approved the sleight of hand Big Al did do;
Must have been a big navigation error;
Credit and praise to the US Air Force,
Who abolished the villagers' death and terror,
Bombing figments of Arc Light Al's imagination,
Re-arranging piles of rock and vegetation.
The ARVNs must have let out a yelp,
Corrupt bastards far beyond all help.
Finally Army Headquarters in Saigon,
Knew what bad stuff was going on.
It was a far better year and day,
When the ARVN had no more say;
Sam, of course, took the bombers away.
In a short time all in all,
Big Al played some very good ball.
He lost one village but saved three,
Could be a record for all history.
He had a conscience and a heart;
You might say the man was smart.

*ARVN – Army of the Republic of Vietnam
* Arc lights – B-52 strikes
* LRRPS – Pronounced lurps, Long Range Recon Patrols
* G-2 – Head intelligence officer

Chapter 5: 1st MIBARS*

Saigon, RVN 1972

Verses (poems) 32 - 34

32. 121 Chi Lang: The Old French
     Colonial Hotel

33. Malingering Ruse de Geurre

34. The Freedom Bird

*1st Military Intelligence Battalion
   Aerial Reconnaissance Support

121 Chi Lang

The red x marks my room on the 2nd floor.

The place was surpassingly groovy;
We had girls, a bar, and a movie.

ONE TWO ONE CHI LANG:
THE OLD FRENCH COLONIAL HOTEL

One two one Chi Lang, I'm here to tell
Was a Shangri-la surrounded by hell.
Only a short way from the presidential palace,
In a Saigon teeming with strife and malice,
The headquarters of the 1st MIBARS*.
Some nights we'd see the moon and stars.
How we lived up north was a war crime,
All covered in sweat, dirt and grime.
Not one officer was a dingleberry*;
On the roof was a big library.
Downstairs was a theater and club,
Our meeting place and social hub.
After six months near the DMZ*,
I felt like a celebrity.
We listened to Elvis and Paul Anka,
Had ceiling fans like in "Casablanca".
Two men in a room with a hot shower;
We spent many a happy off-duty hour.
Jack Hoffman from Tucson, Arizona
Was gregarious and never a loner.
When we called him "off" for short,
Always he had a profane retort.
Ethnic cleansing was a girl and a bar of soap;
A hell of a lot better than old Bob Hope.
My roomie wore a peace symbol and a boonie hat;
Jack had a 'stache' and a big roll of fat,

A dope-smoking-peace-mongering Democrat.
Rheumy Jack with coke bottle glasses,
Really loved the local lasses.
Jack and I were beaucoup mop;*
Our food not mess hall army slop.
No one ever about the chow was bitchin';
We had gourmet cooks in the hotel kitchen.
The place was surpassingly groovy;
We had girls, a bar, and a movie.
After chow almost every single day,
I helped Sergeant Thompkins put the flags away.
We took down and folded Old Glory;
With the gook flag it was another story.
Like wise men who came from afar,
We stached the flags behind the bar.
Everyday at precisely six-thirty,
The girls arrived and things got dirty.
Sitting on Hondas driven by pimps,
They had the time to preen and primp.
The boys had fun, now don't you know?
The girls were two thirty-eight a throw.
One evening I heard the battle alarm;
I hoped no one would buy the farm.
Rushing to the arms room for my M-16,
I was more scared than feeling mean.
Jack jumped off the belly of his whore;
His feet hitting the hard tile floor.
His battle station was next to me;
He arrived late a minute or three.
Only a drill no one came to harm.

Roomie Jack was out of uniform.
I went downstairs for another beer.
Jack was gone and out of here.
Already he had paid his money;
Back to the room to finish his honey.
A haven for youthful debauchery;
In the home of the brave and the land of the free;
Nothing quite like it, I'll ever see.
I had already a degree from college;
Now a degree in carnal knowledge.
After ninety days in the old hotel,
It was time to leave that horrid hell.
For another year and a half,
Under Army rule I'd chafe.
No matter how much you're thrilled;
It's still too easy to be killed.
People say thanks for your service;
Shooting wars still make me nervous.
Be sure the candle is worth the game,*
Before troops are sent and wars proclaimed.

* 121 Chi Lang – street address of the hotel
* MIBARS – Military Intelligence Battalion Aerial
  Reconnaissance Support
* Dingleberry – piece of crap
* DMZ – demilitarized zone
* Beaucoup mop – very fat
* Game – count the cost (one of Ben Franklin's sayings)

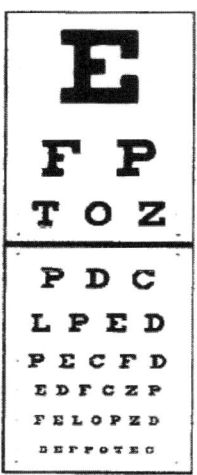

Not having a license to drive,

Increased my chances of staying alive.

With a license I'd be at their beck and call,

Not resting completely at night at all.

MALINGERING RUSE de GUERRE*

Any extra duty I liked not a damn,
Considering I'd been screwed over by Sam.
I recall with considerable pride
The old warrant officer's ride,
To the airstrip at Phu Bai.
He prayed to God he would not be killed
'Til over the DMZ he could be drilled.
You signed your license and you could drive;
No written, eye tests or other jive.
In Saigon it was quite another matter;
Officers wanted not their blood to splatter.
Not having a license to drive,
Increased my chances of staying alive.
With a license I'd be at their beck and call,
Not resting completely at night at all.
Not smart enough to try OCS*,
I'd be too blind for the eye test.
With some knowledge of lenses and such,
To fool Sam's minions didn't take much.
With my bad not dominant eye,
I pretended to give the machine a try.
I read down two lines and quits;
They bought it all, the stupid shits.
Screw you simple bastard Sam;
No more driving for me in the Nam.
There was no complaining or gripes;

I was driven around by a sergeant with 3 more stripes.
I felt so safe and sound;
He knew well his way around.

* OCS – Officers Candidate School
* Ruse de Guerre – A trick to deceive the enemy

THE FREEDOM BIRD

It was time to be off and away;
I served in Nam nine months to the day.
We boarded a huge silver jet plane,
The designation of which escapes my brain.
The stewardesses were blond and tall
But we liked the cool air best of all.
I choose a good window seat,
Offering views surpassingly neat.
I saw many a coral atoll
More than five miles below.
I spent nine months in a war zone;
Three years my Dad from home was gone.
He told me a little about Bogainville;
How he was abandoned by the Navy
And adopted by the Marines,
Sharing their tobacco, bullets and beans;
Helping Japs for their emperor to die
Who attacked by day shouting "BANSAI"!
For self preservation – never asking why.
Hours later with night enveloping the land,
To refuel we landed in Kyoto, Japan;
Many hours later we landed in Anchorage,
Stepping off the plane and into a fridge.
Not all were happy to be in the USA;
Some had wives and children far away,
Left to war and with hell to pay.

Some had a far away vacant stare,
With pain just too much to bear.
On a headset I listened to tunes;
The ordeal could not be over too soon.
It was another crashing bore,
Landing on the California shore.
Herded onto a green Army bus;
Enough to make a preacher cuss;
Off then to the Army's Presidio;
We had no choice but to go,
For a new issue of Army duds;
I hated them all – the sorry cruds.
Finally, to Atlanta I did fly,
Leaving California no tears to the eye.
Sometime about half past eleven,
Landing in Tennessee our 727.
Mom, Dad and my little brother Jack
Were waiting there to welcome me back.
It was indeed my very first car;
To pick it up we drove not far,
A few miles southward to Maryville town
To where my lime – colored lemon was found.
So easy to drive and light on gas;
Rapid enough to really haul ass;
It was a lemon through and through,
A six-banger Plymouth Duster model '72.
For a while it made me nervous;
Just Detroit's way of saying
Screw you, dude, for your service.

Chapter 6: 1st MIBARS*

Fort Bragg, North Carolina 1972 – 1973

Verses (poems) 35 – 38

35. The Medal

36. First Sergeant Cooper at Fort Bragg

37. The Purple Flashlight

38. Guard Mount

*Military Intelligence Battalion Aerial
   Reconnaissance Support

I interpreted (readout)

SR-71 imagery at

Fort Bragg, North Carolina

For several classified projects.

THE GEORGE WASHINGTON FREEDOM MEDAL

THE MEDAL

Escaped from the Nam to Fort Bragg;
Army life was but a painful drag.
On the battalion bulletin board I chanced to see
An essay contest – just my cup of tea,
Sponsored by The Freedoms Foundation at Valley Forge,
A singular honor with letters writ large.
It caught my eye the 1st Grand Prize;
What I'd do with $1500 I could surmise.
And a George Washington Action Play Set,
With a flag and a medal you can bet.
What are you doing? The section chief asked.
I responded with a show of brass.
I'm going to win that essay prize,
When I do don't be surprised;
He looked at me, smiled, and rolled his eyes.
I said in truth with no modesty,
I won first place in Tennessee,
A contest sponsored by the FOP*,
"What Law Enforcement Means to my Community",
Seeking understanding and some immunity.
I won a scholarship and a trophy for my school;
I'm pretty good as a general rule.
"Freedom Has a Price" was the theme,
In a 1000 words or even less,
Was the cardinal rule of the contest.
I used the best materials that I had;

A blue ink pen and a yellow pad.
I expected to win but didn't hold my breath;
A lot can go wrong in an essay contest.
In about a month after the deadline,
We got a surprise that was not all mine.
Quitting early for a battalion formation,
My puzzlement soon turned to mild elation.
In front of the barracks of Company A,
It was indeed the place where I did stay;
In three ranks the whole battalion was there,
Like a freak show at a county fair.
Someone told me what it was all about;
The glorious sight had removed all doubt,
With the men there standing at ease;
Flags and guidons* painting the breeze.
My own horn I did not have to toot;
The lieutenant colonel returned my salute,
Reflecting credit and honor on the service;
The Medal of Honor it was surely not,
But the The Freedoms Medal did salve a spot;
Helping not my toes nor the jungle rot.
Freedom, indeed, has a steep price,
With side effects much less than nice.

*FOP – Fraternal Order of Police
* guidons – flags carried for unit identification

FIRST SERGEANT COOPER AT FORT BRAGG

He was a red headed Michigander;
It seems that I was his pet goose;
My military standards were just too loose.
Every Wednesday formation he'd single me out;
I took it like a man – didn't sulk or pout.
His job was to harass me – he did really good;
To me he was a lifer – a red headed peckerwood.
One week I wore unstarched clothes,
Disturbing his equilibrium and breaking his nose;
It was a breach of national security,
To get a fresh costume – he gave me three;
I changed my shirt exactly as he told.
When I returned not insubordinate or bold,
He was apoplectic I had on the pants old.
His ruddy face was redder still,
'Til my fresh pants filled the bill;
Meanwhile the company's skinny clerk,
The fawning sycophantic jerk,
Wrote the offenses down beside my name.
No soldier of the month a crying shame,
But I had some other compensation;
Pro pay* and a medal from The Freedoms Foundation
Reflecting great credit on the service and me,
Sustaining until home in Tennessee.
He did his job I was a slob;
Army life was not my cup of tea.

A smarter version of Gomer Pyle?
Our repartee made the others smile.

* Pro pay - $100 a month for proficiency

THE PURPLE FLASHLIGHT

The first sergeant was getting at me back,
Rubbing turpentine on my scrotum and crack*.
My uniforms weren't up to snuff,
Nor my shaves nearly close enough.
A month more I must endure,
Then I'd be gone and out of here.
It was guilt by close association;
Big Al was proving to be my salvation,
A plant to guide me aright,
And not embarrass the battalion that Saturday night.
Big Al was my very best friend;
We hung together to the bitter end.
It will go very hard with you,
If you let Noland upward screw,
Saith the battalion sergeant major unto Al.
To guard the airfield was our task;
We were volunteered and never asked.
There were hippies alleged to be in town;
They might use a flag to burn Fort Bragg down.
We had brought our basic soldier gear
And were given flashlights to serve here.
There was just a single line you see;
Al was, of course, standing next to me.
Nothing gives officers such huge erections
As performing all the prescribed inspections.
He was the lieutenant officer of the guard
With a humorless look severe and hard.

Why is your flashlight purple and the others green?
A question that struck me as stupid and obscene;
I was part of a conspiracy to wreck the nation,
Aided by the purple flashlight's illumination.
I wanted to crush his windpipe and stomp his stupid face,
But I kept my cool and stayed in my place.
I saw him but he wasn't there,
Lost in space with my one-thousand-yard stare.
I said aloud in a dull monotone,
I asked for bread and they gave me a stone;
It was a thing that Jesus did say,
So he left me alone the rest of the day,
The situation that he soon assessed,
With crazy people you should not mess.

* Scrotum and crack — treatment meted out to unwanted stray
dogs by mountain people.

GUARD MOUNT

I was a short-timer with only a week;
My growing excitement was about to peak;
My problem didn't seem all that large;
Just one more pay back from the first sarge.
It was only in prolonged retrospect,
I figured out he was giving me heck;
A cowardly Army sucker sneak.
Maybe it was only a trick of a feeble mind;
The officers seemed to like my work just fine.
It was those mythological hippies again.
They might just do the aircraft in.
Another formation for close inspection,
To give enlisted trash needed direction.
Specialist Noland, what's your first general order?
I left the reservation and over the border.
The officer of the guard thought me a commie whore,
Almost a civilian I'd play Army no more.
I will walk my post in a military manner
And take no shit from the company commander!
His veins popped out and his eyes did twitch;
I thought he'd stroke out – that son of a bitch.

WHAT DID YOU SAY?

I will walk my post in a military manner
And quit my post only when properly relieved, SIR.

It was Al's fault you must understand;
Letting me be insolent to that nice young man.
He gave Al a hateful glare,
For being born and standing there.
It was two on and two off,*
Try it first before you scoff.
Sleepily I was leaning against a LOACH;*
Luckily no one else did then approach.
I'd be damned committing a mortal sin;
The whole damn side of the thing caved in.
It was only thin plexiglass,
But still enough to cook my ass.
It was enough to scare me awake;
I'd be more careful, for goodness sake.
I told Al where he must keep away
And back in character my role to play.
The last battle of the war I'd fight,
A poor way to spend Saturday night.

* Guard duty for two hours – sleep for two hours
* LOACH – light observation helicopter

Chapter 7: Aftermath

Home In Tennessee 1973 – 2018

Verses (poems) 39 - 42

HOMEWARD BOUND

I had paid my debt to society,
After 3 years and 8 days I was free.
Gazing at Bragg in the rearview mirror,
Each passing second brought home nearer.
It was over an 8 hour trek;
I had a lot of time to reflect.
Random thoughts popped into my head,
Grateful I was not crippled or dead.
My friend who lived next to me
Had crashed and burned in the DMZ,
Killing any lingering desire to fly.
I wiped a tear or two from my eye.
Nixon was drowning in the Watergate mess,
Great entertainment for me I confess;
It couldn't happen to a nicer despot,
Unless we could shoot Lyndon on the spot.
My hearing was so much worse,
Temper short and mood perverse.
I learned somewhat to compensate;
I'd stand close and on lips concentrate.
I knew not about PTSD at the time;
You better not grab me from behind;
I'd bust you up and lose my mind.
I was too stupid to be very nervous;
I preferred Vietnam to Fort Bragg Service.
The Army in Nam left me to my work;

My expertise for me was a perk.
I managed to avoid Sam's booby traps,
But at Bragg too much Mickey Mouse crap.
Listening to Casey Kasem's* Top 40,
I cruised westward bound on I-40.
It was early December in the late fall;
The weather was chilly with no leaves at all.
Out of the Army I was overjoyed.
Then I realized I was not employed.
I needed time to let my mind rest,
To plan for me what was best.
I'd go back for teacher certification
And be useful to myself, state, and nation.
It was dark when I got home;
I had supper and a big corn pone.
Mother was glad to have me back;
Peanut butter cookies I had for a snack.
I took out my telescope and looked at Orion;
Things were going to be really just fine.
For billions of others and not just me,
God made place, space, and eternity;
All that ever was or will ever be;
For my deliverance, Lord, I thank thee.

* Casey Kasem – a very popular radio personality of yesteryear.

IN MEMORIUM

ELIZABETH CLAIBORNE NOLAND

Jan 5	Oct 20
1939	2017

She lifted me up never put me down,
The most loving woman I could've found.
She was compassionate, beautiful, and smart,
Loving me always with all her heart.

ELEGY TO ELIZABETH: BIRTHDAY SURPRISE

It was the end of the school year;
A memory ever most dear.
I'd paid for it – but it was free,
So conventional wisdom said to me;
A credit union end of the year deal,
A Friday night right good meal.
I remember not a word that was said;
Remembering only that I was well fed.
We both were about to homeward start,
When finally I did something smart;
Without hesitation or purpose of evasion,
I struck up a lively conversation.
I saw before me a lovely face,
With every auburn hair in place.
I got her number and a date;
She pleased didn't hesitate.
Thanks to prayers offered by Mother,
It seems we were made for each other.
We met on her father's birthday,
Information she soon did say.
In two months we were happily married;
Our love never, ever miscarried.
She lifted me up never put me down,
The most loving woman I could've found.
Our forty years far too soon did pass,
But my memories will forever last.
She was compassionate, beautiful, and smart,
Loving me always with all her heart.
We met at the right time and the right spot;
Serendipitous was that parking lot.

It was on a hot October day;
She breathed her last and passed away.
I thought I'd die from the suffocating grief;
To the VA* clinic I went for relief.
They wanted me to take up hobbies,
When for tranquilizers I did lobby.
I got no government relief that day.
I cursed them under my breath and went away.
My family doc prescribed an adequate supply,
So 24/7 I wouldn't grieve, sob, and cry.
For you this must always be hearsay;
I saw her on the 131st day,
After she had passed on-away;
A beautiful, radiant apparition,
In a most happy and healthful condition.
From only 30 feet away,
She made my life and my day.
I gave her my undivided attention;
She was in full color I must mention,
Clad in hot pink and gleaming white;
It was in mid morn, not at night.
She had no pockets or jewelry,
Nor lines in her face that I could see.
I had a new life starting that day;
Most of my grief melted away.
She kept eye contact always smiling;
It was her spirit no evil beguiling.
In 30 seconds or less she was gone,
But in my memory she lingers on;
She took my fears and doubts away,
Restored my faith what's more to say?
The first and last time I saw her face
Were both displays of God's loving grace.

The one thing I'd really like to know,
How did she manage a heavenly furlough?
She was holy in the Catholic sense;
Must be her – not my just recompense.

*VA – Veterans Administration

CHICKEN HAWKS

They talk the talk;
Walk not the walk;
Not Screaming Eagles,
Just chicken hawks.*
They beat their chests and drums;
Watch the news and suck their thumbs,
And like to cluck and squawk;
They're not patriots at all,
But craven chicken hawks.
Every intervention they say is so good;
They'd join the military if only they could;
When so much younger they wouldn't serve,
Was it good sense or lack of nerve?
Too rich and clever for the draft,
They profiteered — the poor got the shaft.
Now our warriors are really volunteers;
Their loss still engenders heartfelt tears,
From their families who are but few;
Chicken hawks run the House and Senate too.
All those crazy foreign wars,
Worthless like shootouts in local bars;
Bravely they shed other's blood,
Their lives fulfilled, things are good.
With special rights they're instilled;
No sons or daughters combat killed.
Why do veterans put these people in office,
Who bait us, switch us, and scoff us?

* Chicken hawks — pro-war people who have not served

Julius Caesar   by William Shakespeare

Act III : SC I, 108 - 110

Brutus:

Then walk we forth, even to the market-place,

And, waving our red weapons o'er our heads,

Let's all cry, 'Peace, freedom and liberty!'

PARTING SHOT

I think of Vietnam almost every day;
Time has not mellowed what I say;
We were the best of our generation,
Victims of the greed of our nation;
We weren't fighting for our democracy;
It was all an illusion you must see.
Our elections were rigged long ago,
By the Founding Fathers who wanted it so.
It is a lie and an awful slander;
No democracy exists with gerrymander.
It's minority rule for the very rich;
Their money and our brains have been laundered;
The future and dreams of the middle class squandered.
Anything short of a nuclear holocaust
Is gainful – an acceptable loss.
We feared the falling of dominoes,
Communist plots and deadly woes;
Not really a war – just a token;
We were gone for Sam had spoken.
Our own people are still dying
And our government always lying.
Now they have their communist paradise;
To interfere was never ever wise.
Their economy is better – not great;
I wish them well – I have no hate.
Should it matter a whit to a fool,
Whether the Sunni or the Shia' rule?

I'm worried about our right to be free;
Freedom is slipping and may not always be.
Will we wonder where it all went;
No free press or right to dissent?

D. A. NOLAND

Aug. 23 *Dec. 19*

1923 *1994*

Thanks, Dad, for your service.

You will always be my hero.

READERS' REACTIONS

AL FUERST

"I first met Garry on a hot dusty day in Phu Bai. I was just out of Screaming Eagle Replacement School (SERTS). I soon learned that Garry was a unique individual. He could converse about astronomy and shift to English Literature in a second. His dry wit could make the most unpleasant situations bearable with a joke or two. Garry hated the Army and the war but was always ready to do what he could to protect the soldier. We became friends and that friendship has lasted these many years after the Army.

This book has allowed him to overcome his PTSD and the loss of his dear wife Libby. It is humor, sadness, and duty all wrapped up together! The stories are all true put into rhyme. I believe this is a unique format for recollections of the war – a unique book – just like Garry."

- Al Fuerst aka Big Al or Arc Light Al

DONNA KELLEY

"Reading these amazing stories told in verse was almost like a Vietnam documentary as told by an exceptional man!

Being raised and an 'Air Force brat' once married to a Vietnam vet, I can relate to your stories. Your style of writing brings to mind a blend of Faulkner and Kipling. Your words so carefully chosen in verse stirred me as a reader to experience so many emotions of your Army experience.

Well done Garry Noland, and thank you for your service!"

- Donna Kelley

TOM MERCER

"These poems that Garry has written gives you a sense of Wow, did he just say that? That's what makes them so damn good. You might think you understand, but then you start thinking, and you have to read them over again.

I like the introduction and how he honors his father. He and his father thought a lot alike, when it comes to the Vietnam War, or police action as the government called it. Only the men fighting knew it was a war and a stupid war to say the least. These poems put all this in the right place. If you read it more than once you may get it and may not.

Big Al is a favorite person Garry talks about a lot. Funny, brave and don't give a shit attitude. He talks about him and Al getting into trouble, which is what men do in a war zone when they get bored.

Fragging the Captain was great. I won't say too much about it. I don't want to give it away; read and get your own opinion about the poem. Me, being a grunt, I loved it. Some officers deserved what they got from the men, being they were pricks sometime to their men.

These poems are from the heart of the author. His feelings and his wording are great and gives you more than just a poem; you get a story if you read it right. Stay on your toes, because you will be puzzled when you read, that's what makes it worth buying.

I can understand the poems, mainly because I was a grunt, but each poem can have more than one, two or three meanings. Garry wants you to figure it out and put your own meaning to the poem.

I want to wish Garry lots of success with this collection of poems, which for some Vets, will bring back good and bad memories. For me it helps me to deal with my P.T.S.D. A laugh always helps."

- Tom Mercer – Vietnam 1967 - 1968

1st Battalion 18th Infantry – Big Red One – Charlie Company

Lima Platoon – Point man, squad and platoon leader

Silver Star – Two Bronze Stars, one with V for valor

CIB – Jump Wings – Valorous unit citation

RALPH P. DAY

"Garry Noland is a very ingenious and gifted writer. In particular he is a seasoned war poet, a devoted soldier and patriot who brilliantly captured what life was like along the hazardous front lines of war torn Vietnam 50 years ago. Somehow over the past year he created a remarkable collection of war poems – blunt and awful yet often humorous and entertaining. In each poem is evidence of his bravery and that of fellow soldiers while their military and political leaders made stupid decisions. In 1971, the year that Noland served in Vietnam, casualties continued to mount, the war was considered unwinnable and back home support was falling rapidly.

Noland's distinct contribution to the Vietnamese war literature is his collection of 42 poems in couplet form. Noland's intimate and candid writing style engages the reader to be present in the jungles of Vietnam with the young American draftees and the tenacious North Vietnamese soldiers. Noland consistently shows his commitment to patriotism and the American cause. His poems are smartly complemented by his own 21 sketches and 5 photos.

Two especially poignant poems praise his closest Army friend Al and his late and deeply loved wife Elizabeth..."

- Ralph P. Day

Lieutenant U.S. Air Force 1960 -1963, retired adjunct professor at Drexel University, Philadelphia, PA.

ED WISEMAN

"*VIETNAM IN VERSE* by Garry Noland is truly a creative masterpiece that rarely comes along. His poetry brings to life the conflicting emotions experienced by the young soldiers. His poetry puts you there with him; his stories become your memories."

- Ed Wiseman
Air Force Reconnaissance
Viet Nam 1960 – 1964

DICK CLEWELL

"This collection of poems by Vietnam veteran Garry Noland vividly captures the remembrances, feelings and reflections of many men and women who served their country well in that ill-conceived encounter. The irony, the gallows humor, and the realization of the 'fickle finger of fate' attached to this futile endeavor again reinforces the hard-won wisdom that going to war for positions of power and economic gain at the expense of the powerless is futility. Warfare should always be the very last option when all other attempts to solve differences have been exhausted."

- Dick Clewell, former Army Chaplain (Vietnam 1966-67) and Chaplain to the Center for Stress Recovery, Brecksville VA Medical Center (1982-96)

ACKNOWLEDGEMENTS

At critical junctures, I had quality help and motivation to undertake and complete this legacy project. Thanks are in order.

Thanks to:

The mercy and grace of God that I survived my ordeal.

Al Fuerst who saved our lives twice within a 36 hour period.

Mary Jo Keshock who became the chief consultant for every aspect of this mini-tome. Her peerless people skills were indispensable.

Ralph P. Day, a nonpareil consultant, for providing many invaluable suggestions and his reactions to my poetic endeavor.

Number one fan Pauline Skabar for her deep appreciation of my work.

Lifelong friend, LTC James Cannon USAF retired, for his encouragement and copying skills.

Elizabeth Vance for copying artwork.

Mary Beth Switzer for the initial typing of the manuscript.

Sandra Hurley for her production of the final manuscript and illustrations.

Former Marine and Vietnam Veteran James Kennedy for his encouragement.

James, Jan, and Cady Moore for their encouragement and friendship.

THANKS FOR READERS' REACTIONS:

AL FUERST
DONNA KELLEY
TOM MERCER
RALPH P. DAY
ED WISEMAN
DICK CLEWELL